EMMANUEL JOSEPH

Coded Cuisine, The Intersection of Robotics, Sociology, and the Art of Cooking

Copyright © 2025 by Emmanuel Joseph

All rights reserved. No part of this publication may be reproduced, stored or transmitted in any form or by any means, electronic, mechanical, photocopying, recording, scanning, or otherwise without written permission from the publisher. It is illegal to copy this book, post it to a website, or distribute it by any other means without permission.

First edition

This book was professionally typeset on Reedsy.
Find out more at reedsy.com

Contents

1. Chapter 1: A New Era in the Kitchen — 1
2. Chapter 2: The Rise of Robotic Chefs — 3
3. Chapter 3: Social Impacts of Automation in Cooking — 5
4. Chapter 4: The Technological Marvels Behind Robotic Cooking — 7
5. Chapter 5: Ethics and Robotics in the Culinary World — 9
6. Chapter 6: The Future of Home Cooking — 11
7. Chapter 7: Culinary Education in the Age of Robots — 13
8. Chapter 8: The Role of AI in Personalized Nutrition — 15
9. Chapter 9: The Art of Cooking in a Tech-Driven World — 17
10. Chapter 10: Robotics and Sustainable Cooking — 19
11. Chapter 11: The Global Impact of Robotic Cuisine — 21
12. Chapter 12: Embracing the Future of Food — 23
13. Chapter 13: The Integration of AI in Culinary Arts Education — 25
14. Chapter 14: The Role of Robotics in Food Safety — 27
15. Chapter 15: The Intersection of Culinary Arts and AI-Driven... — 29
16. Chapter 16: Robotics and the Future of Food Production — 31
17. Chapter 17: The Human Element in a Robotic Culinary World — 33

1

Chapter 1: A New Era in the Kitchen

The kitchen, once considered the heart of the home, has undergone dramatic transformations throughout history. From the open fires of ancient civilizations to the sleek, modern designs of contemporary homes, the evolution of the kitchen is a reflection of societal progress. In recent years, the infusion of advanced technology, particularly robotics, has propelled this evolution to unprecedented heights. The advent of smart appliances, automated cooking devices, and AI-driven kitchen assistants is revolutionizing how we prepare, cook, and even think about food.

At the core of this transformation is the fusion of robotics and artificial intelligence. These technologies are enabling machines to perform tasks that were once the sole domain of humans, such as chopping vegetables, monitoring cooking temperatures, and even plating dishes with artistic precision. This intersection of robotics and culinary arts is not just about convenience; it's about pushing the boundaries of what is possible in the kitchen. It challenges traditional notions of cooking and opens up new possibilities for creativity and efficiency.

From a sociological perspective, the rise of robotic kitchens is also reshaping the dynamics of domestic life. The roles and responsibilities associated with food preparation are shifting, as families adapt to a new reality where machines can take on many of the labor-intensive tasks. This shift has implications for gender roles, as the kitchen has historically been a space where traditional gender norms are both reinforced and challenged. The integration of robotics in the kitchen could potentially redistribute these roles in more equitable ways.

Moreover, the cultural significance of cooking is being redefined. Food has always been a powerful symbol of identity, tradition, and community. As robots become more prevalent in the kitchen, questions arise about the preservation of culinary heritage and the authenticity of robot-prepared meals. However, rather than diminishing the cultural value of cooking, robotics has the potential to enhance it by making it more accessible and by preserving traditional techniques in digital form.

2

Chapter 2: The Rise of Robotic Chefs

In professional kitchens, the introduction of robotic chefs is changing the culinary landscape. These advanced machines, equipped with precision and consistency, are capable of executing complex recipes with a level of accuracy that even the most skilled human chefs can find challenging. Robotic arms that can flip burgers, stir sauces, and garnish plates are becoming increasingly common in high-end restaurants and fast-food chains alike.

One of the primary advantages of robotic chefs is their ability to maintain consistent quality. Human chefs, while highly skilled, can experience fluctuations in performance due to fatigue, stress, or other factors. Robots, on the other hand, can work tirelessly for extended periods without any decline in efficiency. This consistency is particularly valuable in environments where precision is paramount, such as molecular gastronomy or fine dining establishments where presentation and taste must be flawless.

The integration of robotic chefs also has economic implications. While the initial investment in robotic technology can be substantial, the long-term savings in labor costs and increased efficiency can lead to significant financial benefits. For restaurants, this means the potential to reduce overhead costs while maintaining high standards of service. Additionally, robotic chefs can operate around the clock, enabling businesses to extend their hours of operation and cater to a broader customer base.

However, the rise of robotic chefs is not without its challenges. There are concerns about the impact on employment in the culinary industry, as robots begin to take over tasks traditionally performed by human workers. This raises important questions about the future of work and the need for policies that address the displacement of labor. At the same time, there is a growing recognition that robots and humans can work together in complementary ways, with robots handling repetitive tasks and humans focusing on creative and strategic aspects of cooking.

3

Chapter 3: Social Impacts of Automation in Cooking

The widespread adoption of automation in cooking is having profound social impacts. One of the most significant changes is the way people interact with food and each other. In households where robotic assistants are taking on cooking duties, there is a shift in how family members engage with meal preparation and dining. This shift has the potential to strengthen family bonds, as individuals have more time to spend together during meals without the stress of cooking.

For busy professionals and families, robotic cooking assistants offer a convenient solution to the challenges of meal preparation. These devices can be programmed to prepare meals at specific times, ensuring that dinner is ready when everyone comes home. This convenience is particularly valuable in today's fast-paced world, where time is a precious commodity. By reducing the time and effort required to cook, robots can help alleviate the pressures of daily life and promote a healthier work-life balance.

In addition to convenience, automation in cooking has the potential to address issues of food security and nutrition. Robotic systems can be used to create nutritious and balanced meals, tailored to the specific dietary needs of individuals. This capability is particularly important for vulnerable populations, such as the elderly or those with chronic health conditions, who may struggle to prepare healthy meals on their own. By ensuring access to nutritious food, robots can play a role in improving overall public health.

However, the social impacts of automation in cooking are not entirely positive. There are concerns about the loss of culinary skills and the erosion of cultural traditions associated with cooking. As robots take on more cooking tasks, there is a risk that people will become disconnected from the process of making food. This disconnection could lead to a decline in the appreciation of culinary arts and a loss of valuable knowledge passed down through generations. It is important to find a balance between embracing technology and preserving the cultural significance of cooking.

4

Chapter 4: The Technological Marvels Behind Robotic Cooking

The technology behind robotic cooking is a marvel of modern engineering. At the heart of these systems are advanced sensors and algorithms that enable robots to perform complex tasks with precision and accuracy. These sensors can detect minute changes in temperature, texture, and flavor, allowing robots to make real-time adjustments to cooking processes. This level of precision is essential for achieving consistent results and ensuring the quality of the final dish.

One of the key components of robotic cooking systems is machine learning. Through continuous learning and adaptation, robots can improve their performance over time. By analyzing data from previous cooking sessions, robots can identify patterns and make adjustments to optimize their cooking techniques. This ability to learn and adapt is what sets robotic chefs apart from traditional kitchen appliances, making them true partners in the culinary arts.

In addition to sensors and machine learning, robotic cooking systems rely on sophisticated hardware. Robotic arms equipped with multiple degrees of freedom can mimic the movements of human hands, allowing them to perform tasks such as chopping, stirring, and plating with remarkable dexterity. These robotic arms are often paired with computer vision systems that enable robots to recognize and manipulate different ingredients with precision. This combination of hardware and software allows robots to replicate the actions of human chefs with a high degree of accuracy.

The integration of robotics with other smart kitchen technologies is also driving innovation in cooking. Smart ovens that can communicate with robotic assistants, for example, can automatically adjust cooking times and temperatures based on the progress of a dish. This level of automation not only simplifies the cooking process but also enhances the overall efficiency of the kitchen. As technology continues to advance, the possibilities for robotic cooking are virtually limitless, promising to transform the way we prepare and enjoy food.

5

Chapter 5: Ethics and Robotics in the Culinary World

As robotics becomes more integrated into the culinary world, ethical considerations come to the forefront. One of the primary ethical concerns is the impact on employment. The automation of cooking tasks has the potential to displace a significant number of workers in the food industry, from line cooks to kitchen staff. This displacement raises questions about the responsibility of businesses and policymakers to support workers who may be affected by technological advancements.

There are also ethical questions related to the use of artificial intelligence in cooking. For example, who is responsible if a robot makes a mistake that results in foodborne illness? The issue of accountability becomes complex when machines are involved, as traditional notions of responsibility may not apply. Establishing clear guidelines and regulations for the use of robotics in the kitchen is essential to address these concerns and ensure the safety and well-being of consumers.

Another ethical consideration is the potential for increased inequality. Access to advanced robotic cooking systems may be limited to those who can afford them, potentially exacerbating existing disparities in food access and nutrition. Ensuring that the benefits of robotic cooking are accessible to a wide range of people, regardless of socioeconomic status, is an important goal.

This may involve developing affordable robotic systems or implementing policies that support the equitable distribution of technological resources.

The use of robotics in cooking also raises questions about the preservation of cultural heritage. Food is an integral part of cultural identity, and the methods and techniques used to prepare traditional dishes are often passed down through generations. As robots take on more cooking tasks, there is a risk that these traditional practices may be lost. Balancing the advantages of automation with the need to preserve cultural heritage is a key ethical challenge in the culinary world.

6

Chapter 6: The Future of Home Cooking

The future of home cooking is poised for a revolution, thanks to advancements in robotics and artificial intelligence. Imagine a kitchen where meal preparation is entirely automated, with robotic assistants handling everything from grocery shopping to cooking and cleaning. This vision of the future is becoming increasingly feasible as technology continues to advance at a rapid pace.

In this future kitchen, smart appliances and robotic assistants work seamlessly together to create a highly efficient cooking environment. Refrigerators equipped with sensors can monitor food inventory and automatically reorder supplies when needed. Robotic chefs can prepare meals based on personalized dietary preferences and nutritional requirements, ensuring that every dish is tailored to the individual's needs. This level of automation not only simplifies meal preparation but also promotes healthier eating habits by providing easy access to nutritious meals.

One of the most exciting aspects of the future of home cooking is the potential for increased creativity and experimentation. With the mundane tasks of cooking taken care of by robots, home cooks can focus on exploring new ingredients, techniques, and recipes. This freedom to experiment can lead to the discovery of unique flavor combinations and culinary innovations that might not have been possible in a traditional kitchen setting. Additionally, robotic assistants can provide real-time feedback and suggestions, acting as collaborative partners in the creative process.

Another significant development in the future of home cooking is the integration of virtual reality and augmented reality technologies. These tools can provide immersive cooking experiences, allowing users to virtually explore cuisines from around the world and learn from top chefs without leaving their homes. Imagine stepping into a virtual Italian kitchen to learn the secrets of making authentic pasta from a master chef or participating in a virtual cooking class with friends from different parts of the globe. These experiences can enrich our understanding of global culinary traditions and foster a sense of community and connection.

Moreover, the future of home cooking will likely see a greater emphasis on sustainability and reducing food waste. Robotic systems can help optimize the use of ingredients, ensuring that nothing goes to waste. They can also assist in meal planning and portion control, helping individuals make more environmentally conscious choices. By promoting sustainable practices, robotic cooking technology has the potential to contribute to a more sustainable food system and reduce the environmental impact of our eating habits.

While the future of home cooking holds immense promise, it also presents challenges that must be addressed. As we embrace automation and technological advancements, it is essential to consider the social and cultural implications. Maintaining a balance between convenience and preserving the joy and creativity of cooking is crucial. Ensuring that technological benefits are accessible to all and do not exacerbate existing inequalities is equally important. By navigating these challenges thoughtfully, we can create a future where robotics and culinary arts coexist harmoniously, enhancing our relationship with food and each other.

7

Chapter 7: Culinary Education in the Age of Robots

As robotics and artificial intelligence become more integrated into the culinary world, culinary education is also evolving to keep pace with technological advancements. Traditional cooking schools are incorporating courses on robotics, automation, and AI, preparing the next generation of chefs to work alongside robotic assistants. This shift in education is essential for equipping aspiring chefs with the skills and knowledge needed to thrive in a tech-driven culinary landscape.

In addition to technical skills, culinary education in the age of robots emphasizes the importance of creativity and innovation. While robots can handle repetitive and precise tasks, human chefs bring creativity, intuition, and emotional intelligence to the kitchen. Culinary schools are fostering these qualities by encouraging students to experiment with new ingredients, techniques, and presentation styles. By combining technical proficiency with creative thinking, chefs can leverage robotics to push the boundaries of culinary arts.

Online learning platforms and virtual reality are also transforming culinary education. Aspiring chefs can access high-quality instruction and resources from anywhere in the world, breaking down geographical barriers and democratizing culinary education. Virtual reality allows students to participate in immersive cooking experiences, simulating real-life kitchen environments and providing hands-on training. These technologies enhance the learning experience and provide students with valuable skills that are relevant in today's tech-driven culinary industry.

Furthermore, culinary education is placing a greater emphasis on interdisciplinary learning. Understanding the principles of robotics, computer science, and engineering is becoming increasingly important for chefs who want to work with advanced kitchen technologies. By integrating these disciplines into culinary curricula, schools are preparing students to navigate the complexities of a tech-enhanced culinary world. This interdisciplinary approach not only equips students with technical skills but also fosters a deeper appreciation for the intersection of technology and culinary arts.

8

Chapter 8: The Role of AI in Personalized Nutrition

Artificial intelligence is playing a significant role in revolutionizing personalized nutrition. With the ability to analyze vast amounts of data, AI can create tailored dietary plans that cater to an individual's specific needs, preferences, and health goals. This level of personalization is transforming how we approach nutrition and enabling us to make more informed and health-conscious choices.

One of the key advantages of AI in personalized nutrition is its ability to provide real-time recommendations. By analyzing data from wearable devices, smart kitchen appliances, and health records, AI systems can offer personalized meal suggestions and nutritional advice. For example, if an individual is tracking their activity levels and caloric intake, an AI-powered app can recommend meals that align with their fitness goals. This dynamic and responsive approach to nutrition helps individuals maintain a balanced diet and achieve their health objectives.

AI is also enhancing our understanding of the relationship between food and health. Through data analysis and machine learning, AI can identify patterns and correlations that may not be immediately apparent to humans. This deeper insight into the effects of different foods on the body can lead to the development of more effective dietary interventions and preventative measures. For individuals with specific health conditions, such as diabetes or food allergies, AI can provide tailored guidance to manage their dietary needs more effectively.

In addition to individual benefits, AI-powered personalized nutrition has the potential to impact public health positively. By promoting healthier eating habits and providing access to personalized dietary advice, AI can help address widespread health issues such as obesity, cardiovascular disease, and malnutrition. Public health initiatives can leverage AI to develop targeted interventions and educational campaigns that promote healthy eating at a population level. By harnessing the power of AI, we can work towards a healthier and more nutritionally informed society.

9

Chapter 9: The Art of Cooking in a Tech-Driven World

Despite the advancements in robotics and AI, the art of cooking remains a deeply human endeavor. The creative expression, intuition, and emotional connection that humans bring to the kitchen are irreplaceable. While robots can assist with precision and efficiency, the heart and soul of cooking lie in the hands of human chefs who infuse their dishes with passion and artistry.

In a tech-driven world, the role of the chef is evolving. Rather than being replaced by robots, chefs are becoming orchestrators of a symphony of technology and culinary artistry. By leveraging the capabilities of robotic assistants, chefs can push the boundaries of creativity and innovation. The collaboration between humans and robots in the kitchen creates opportunities for new culinary experiences that captivate the senses and delight the palate.

The art of cooking is also about storytelling. Every dish tells a story, whether it's a reflection of cultural heritage, a celebration of seasonal ingredients, or a personal expression of the chef's creativity. This narrative aspect of cooking is something that robots cannot replicate. Human chefs have the unique ability to convey emotions, memories, and traditions through their dishes, creating a deeper connection with diners.

Furthermore, the sensory experience of cooking and dining is inherently human. The tactile sensation of kneading dough, the aroma of spices wafting through the air, and the satisfaction of savoring a beautifully plated dish are all experiences that resonate on an emotional level. While robots can assist with the technical aspects of cooking, it is the human touch that brings these sensory experiences to life. In a world where technology is ever-present, the art of cooking reminds us of the simple joys and profound connections that food can bring.

10

Chapter 10: Robotics and Sustainable Cooking

The integration of robotics into the culinary world offers exciting possibilities for promoting sustainable cooking practices. With growing awareness of the environmental impact of food production and consumption, there is a pressing need to adopt more sustainable approaches in the kitchen. Robotics can play a pivotal role in this transformation by optimizing resource use, reducing waste, and promoting eco-friendly practices.

One of the ways robotics can contribute to sustainability is through precise portion control and ingredient management. By accurately measuring and dispensing ingredients, robotic systems can minimize food waste and ensure that only the necessary amounts are used. This precision not only helps reduce waste but also enhances the overall efficiency of the cooking process. Additionally, robotic systems can analyze data on ingredient usage and provide insights on how to optimize resource allocation, further contributing to sustainable practices.

Another area where robotics can make a significant impact is in the reduction of energy consumption. Smart kitchen appliances and robotic cooking systems can be programmed to operate at optimal energy levels, minimizing unnecessary energy use. For example, smart ovens can adjust cooking times and temperatures based on the specific requirements of a dish, ensuring that energy is used efficiently. By reducing energy consumption, robotic systems can help lower the carbon footprint of cooking activities and contribute to a more sustainable food system.

Robotics can also support sustainable agriculture by promoting the use of locally sourced and seasonal ingredients. Robotic systems can be integrated with supply chain management tools to track the availability of local produce and recommend recipes that utilize these ingredients. This approach not only supports local farmers and reduces the environmental impact of transportation but also encourages consumers to embrace seasonal eating. By fostering a closer connection between consumers and local food sources, robotics can play a role in building a more sustainable and resilient food system.

11

Chapter 11: The Global Impact of Robotic Cuisine

The impact of robotic cuisine extends beyond individual kitchens and has far-reaching implications on a global scale. As robotics and AI continue to advance, they have the potential to address some of the most pressing challenges in the global food system, including food security, nutrition, and environmental sustainability. By leveraging the capabilities of robotics, we can work towards creating a more equitable and sustainable food future.

One of the key global challenges that robotics can help address is food security. In regions where access to food is limited, robotic systems can be deployed to optimize agricultural practices and increase food production. Precision farming technologies, such as robotic harvesters and automated irrigation systems, can enhance crop yields and reduce the reliance on manual labor. Additionally, robotic systems can assist in the distribution of food, ensuring that it reaches those in need more efficiently and effectively.

Robotics can also play a role in improving global nutrition. By providing access to nutritious and balanced meals, robotic cooking systems can help address malnutrition and dietary deficiencies in vulnerable populations. For example, robots can be programmed to prepare fortified foods that address specific nutritional needs, such as iron-rich meals for individuals with anemia.

This capability is particularly important in developing regions where access to diverse and nutrient-rich foods may be limited.

Furthermore, the global adoption of robotic cuisine can contribute to environmental sustainability by promoting sustainable agricultural practices and reducing food waste. By optimizing resource use and minimizing waste, robotic systems can help mitigate the environmental impact of food production and consumption. This approach is essential for addressing the global challenges of climate change and resource depletion. By embracing robotics, we can work towards a more sustainable and resilient food system that supports both people and the planet.

The global impact of robotic cuisine also extends to cultural exchange and culinary innovation. By providing access to diverse culinary traditions and techniques, robotics can facilitate cross-cultural learning and collaboration. Imagine a world where chefs from different countries can share their knowledge and expertise through robotic platforms, creating a global network of culinary innovation. This exchange of ideas can lead to the development of new and exciting culinary experiences that celebrate the richness of global food culture.

12

Chapter 12: Embracing the Future of Food

As we look to the future, the intersection of robotics, sociology, and the art of cooking holds immense promise. The advancements in technology are transforming how we think about and interact with food, offering new possibilities for creativity, efficiency, and sustainability. By embracing the potential of robotics, we can create a future where food is more accessible, nutritious, and environmentally friendly.

However, it is essential to approach this future with a thoughtful and balanced perspective. While robotics offers numerous benefits, it is crucial to consider the social, cultural, and ethical implications of these advancements. Ensuring that the benefits of robotic cuisine are accessible to all and do not exacerbate existing inequalities is a key priority. By addressing these challenges, we can work towards a more inclusive and equitable food future.

Moreover, it is important to preserve the human connection to food and the cultural significance of cooking. While robots can assist with the technical aspects of cooking, the heart and soul of the culinary arts lie in the hands of human chefs who bring creativity, passion, and storytelling to their dishes. By celebrating this human element, we can ensure that the art of cooking remains a vibrant and essential part of our lives.

The future of food is a collaborative journey that involves the efforts of chefs, technologists, policymakers, and consumers. By working together, we can harness the power of robotics to create a culinary landscape that is innovative, sustainable, and culturally enriching. As we embrace the future of food, let us celebrate the intersection of technology and tradition, and the endless possibilities that lie ahead.

13

Chapter 13: The Integration of AI in Culinary Arts Education

The integration of artificial intelligence into culinary arts education is revolutionizing how future chefs are trained. With AI-driven tools and platforms, culinary students can access personalized learning experiences tailored to their individual needs and learning styles. These tools can provide real-time feedback, track progress, and offer suggestions for improvement, creating a dynamic and interactive learning environment.

One of the key benefits of AI in culinary education is the ability to simulate real-world kitchen scenarios. Virtual reality (VR) and augmented reality (AR) technologies, powered by AI, allow students to practice their skills in a controlled and immersive environment. These simulations can replicate various kitchen setups, from a bustling restaurant kitchen to a home kitchen, providing students with a comprehensive understanding of different culinary contexts.

Moreover, AI can assist in recipe development and experimentation. AI algorithms can analyze vast amounts of data on ingredients, cooking techniques, and flavor profiles to suggest innovative combinations and variations. This capability encourages students to think creatively and push the boundaries of traditional cooking. By leveraging AI, culinary education can foster a culture of innovation and experimentation, preparing students to become trailblazers in the culinary world.

In addition to technical skills, AI-powered educational tools can also help students develop soft skills, such as time management, teamwork, and communication. These skills are essential for success in the culinary industry, where collaboration and efficiency are paramount. AI-driven platforms can facilitate group projects, track individual contributions, and provide insights on how to improve team dynamics. By integrating AI into culinary education, schools can create a holistic learning experience that prepares students for the multifaceted challenges of the culinary world.

14

Chapter 14: The Role of Robotics in Food Safety

Food safety is a critical concern in the culinary industry, and robotics is playing an increasingly important role in ensuring the safety and quality of food. Robotic systems can enhance food safety by performing tasks that require high levels of precision and consistency, reducing the risk of human error. For example, robots can be used to handle raw ingredients, ensuring that they are stored and processed under optimal conditions to prevent contamination.

One of the key advantages of robotics in food safety is the ability to perform continuous monitoring and real-time analysis. Advanced sensors and AI algorithms can detect potential hazards, such as changes in temperature, humidity, or pH levels, and take corrective actions to mitigate risks. This proactive approach to food safety helps prevent issues before they become problems, ensuring that food products meet the highest standards of quality and safety.

Robotics can also improve traceability in the food supply chain. With the ability to track and record data at every stage of the production process, robotic systems can provide a detailed and transparent record of how food is produced, processed, and distributed. This traceability is essential for identifying and addressing potential food safety issues and for ensuring compliance with regulatory standards. By enhancing traceability, robotics can help build consumer trust and confidence in the safety of the food supply.

Moreover, robotics can assist in the implementation of stringent hygiene and sanitation practices. Automated cleaning systems can ensure that kitchen and food processing environments are thoroughly sanitized, reducing the risk of cross-contamination. Robots can also be used to handle tasks that require strict hygiene protocols, such as packaging and sealing food products. By reducing human contact with food, robotics can minimize the risk of contamination and enhance overall food safety.

15

Chapter 15: The Intersection of Culinary Arts and AI-Driven Creativity

The intersection of culinary arts and AI-driven creativity is opening up new possibilities for innovation and experimentation in the kitchen. AI-powered tools and platforms can assist chefs in exploring new flavor combinations, cooking techniques, and presentation styles, pushing the boundaries of traditional culinary arts. This collaboration between humans and AI is transforming how we think about creativity in the culinary world.

One of the ways AI is driving creativity in the kitchen is through the analysis of vast amounts of data on ingredients and recipes. AI algorithms can identify patterns and correlations that may not be immediately apparent to human chefs, suggesting novel combinations and techniques. This data-driven approach to creativity allows chefs to experiment with new ideas and concepts, leading to the discovery of unique and exciting culinary experiences.

AI can also assist in the development of personalized culinary experiences. By analyzing data on individual preferences and dietary needs, AI-powered platforms can create customized menus and recipes tailored to each person's tastes and requirements. This level of personalization enhances the dining experience and allows chefs to connect with their customers on a deeper level. By leveraging AI, chefs can create dishes that resonate with their diners and leave a lasting impression.

Moreover, AI-driven creativity extends to the presentation and plating of dishes. AI algorithms can analyze visual data and suggest aesthetically pleasing arrangements and garnishes, elevating the visual appeal of a dish. This capability is particularly valuable in the world of fine dining, where presentation plays a crucial role in the overall dining experience. By collaborating with AI, chefs can enhance their artistic expression and create visually stunning dishes that captivate the senses.

16

Chapter 16: Robotics and the Future of Food Production

The future of food production is being shaped by advancements in robotics and automation. From farm to table, robotic systems are transforming how food is grown, harvested, processed, and distributed. These technological innovations are addressing some of the most pressing challenges in food production, including labor shortages, resource optimization, and environmental sustainability.

In agriculture, robotics is revolutionizing the way crops are grown and harvested. Autonomous robots equipped with advanced sensors and AI algorithms can perform tasks such as planting, watering, and harvesting with precision and efficiency. These robots can operate around the clock, increasing productivity and reducing the reliance on manual labor. Additionally, robotic systems can optimize resource use, such as water and fertilizers, reducing waste and minimizing the environmental impact of farming practices.

Robotics is also enhancing food processing and packaging. Automated systems can handle tasks such as sorting, grading, and packaging food products with speed and accuracy. This level of automation ensures that food products are processed efficiently and meet consistent quality standards. Moreover, robotic systems can adapt to changes in production volumes and product types, providing flexibility and scalability in food processing operations.

The integration of robotics in the food supply chain is improving the efficiency and transparency of food distribution. Autonomous delivery vehicles and drones can transport food products quickly and efficiently, reducing transportation costs and minimizing the risk of spoilage. Additionally, robotic systems can track and record data at every stage of the supply chain, providing a transparent and traceable record of how food is produced and distributed. This traceability is essential for ensuring food safety and building consumer trust.

As we look to the future, the continued advancement of robotics in food production holds immense potential for addressing global food challenges. By leveraging robotic technologies, we can create a more sustainable, efficient, and resilient food system that supports the growing demands of a rapidly expanding global population.

17

Chapter 17: The Human Element in a Robotic Culinary World

In a world where robotics and automation are becoming increasingly prevalent, the human element remains essential in the culinary arts. While robots can handle tasks that require precision and efficiency, it is the creativity, intuition, and emotional connection that humans bring to the kitchen that makes cooking a deeply meaningful and fulfilling experience.

One of the key roles of human chefs in a robotic culinary world is to provide the creative vision and artistic expression that defines culinary arts. Chefs bring their unique perspectives, experiences, and cultural influences to their dishes, creating culinary masterpieces that reflect their individuality. This creative expression is something that robots cannot replicate, as it is deeply rooted in the human experience and imagination.

Human chefs also play a crucial role in fostering a sense of community and connection through food. Cooking and sharing meals is a fundamental aspect of human culture, bringing people together and creating lasting memories. Chefs have the ability to create dining experiences that evoke emotions, tell stories, and celebrate traditions. This sense of connection and community is an integral part of the culinary arts and is something that robots cannot replace.

Moreover, the human element is essential in providing personalized and empathetic service in the culinary industry. While robots can assist with technical tasks, it is the human touch that creates a warm and welcoming dining experience. Chefs and restaurant staff can anticipate and respond to the needs and preferences of their customers, providing a level of care and attention that goes beyond what robots can offer. This human interaction is a key component of the hospitality industry and is vital for creating memorable dining experiences.

As we embrace the advancements in robotics and automation, it is important to recognize and celebrate the unique contributions of human chefs. By combining the precision and efficiency of robots with the creativity and emotional intelligence of humans, we can create a culinary world that is innovative, inclusive, and deeply enriching.

In **Coded Cuisine: The Intersection of Robotics, Sociology, and the Art of Cooking**," embark on a fascinating journey through the culinary world transformed by advanced robotics and artificial intelligence. This book delves deep into the technological marvels behind robotic cooking, the social impacts of automation, and the ethical considerations that arise. It explores how robotic chefs are revolutionizing professional kitchens, enhancing food safety, and promoting sustainable practices.

The book also sheds light on the evolving landscape of culinary education, where AI-driven tools are shaping the next generation of chefs. With chapters on personalized nutrition, the future of home cooking, and the global impact of robotic cuisine, "Coded Cuisine" presents a comprehensive view of how technology is redefining our relationship with food. Through a blend of creativity, precision, and cultural insights, this book celebrates the unique contributions of both human chefs and robotic assistants, offering a glimpse into a future where culinary arts and technology harmoniously coexist.

www.ingramcontent.com/pod-product-compliance
Lightning Source LLC
LaVergne TN
LVHW020457080526
838202LV00057B/6009